Forces and Motion

Lesley Evans Ogden

MEDIA ENHANCED BOOKS
AV2 BY WEIGL
ADDED VALUE · AUDIO VISUAL

www.av2books.com

AV² provides enriched content that supplements and complements this book. Weigl's AV² books strive to create inspired learning and engage young minds in a total learning experience.

Your AV² Media Enhanced books come alive with...

Audio
Listen to sections of the book read aloud.

Key Words
Study vocabulary, and complete a matching word activity.

Go to **www.av2books.com**, and enter this book's unique code.

Video
Watch informative video clips.

Quizzes
Test your knowledge.

BOOK CODE

Q516851

Embedded Weblinks
Gain additional information for research.

Slide Show
View images and captions, and prepare a presentation.

AV² by Weigl brings you media enhanced books that support active learning.

Try This!
Complete activities and hands-on experiments.

... and much, much more!

Published by AV² by Weigl
350 5th Avenue, 59th Floor
New York, NY 10118
Website: www.av2books.com   www.weigl.com

Library of Congress Cataloging-in-Publication Data

Evans Ogden, Lesley J. (Lesley Joan), 1968-
Forces and Motion / Lesley Evans Ogden.
    p. cm. -- (Physical science)
Includes bibliographical references and index.
ISBN 978-1-61690-729-7 (hardcover : alk. paper) -- ISBN 978-1-61690-733-4 (softcover : alk. paper)
1. Force and energy--Juvenile literature. 2. Motion--Juvenile literature. I. Title.
QC73.4.E94 2012
531'.11--dc22
                            2011002295

Printed in the United States of America in North Mankato, Minnesota
1 2 3 4 5 6 7 8 9 0 15 14 13 12 11

052011
WEP37500

Project Coordinator Aaron Carr
Design Terry Paulhus

Every reasonable effort has been made to trace ownership and to obtain permission to reprint copyright material. The publishers would be pleased to have any errors or omissions brought to their attention so that they may be corrected in subsequent printings.

Weigl acknowledges Getty Images as its primary image supplier for this title.

CONTENTS

AV² Code 2

Studying Forces and Motion 5

The Force of Gravity 6

Frictional Forces 8

Describing Motion .10

Gravity and Planetary Motion 12

First Law of Motion 14

Second Law of Motion 17

Third Law of Motion 18

What is a Physicist? 19

Six Facts About Forces and Motion 20

Forces and Motion Brain Teasers 21

Science in Action 22

Words to Know/Index 23

Log on to www.av2books.com 24

Some places in the ocean have fast-flowing water currents. These currents are caused by the **tide** going in and out. The energy from this fast-moving water can be captured and turned into electricity using underwater **turbines**. Tidal power is a source of **renewable energy**. Unlike fuels such as coal and oil, tidal power will not run out. This is because the change in tide is a result of forces caused by movements of the Sun and Moon.

Studying Forces and Motion

Force refers to the action of pushing or pulling something. Forces can cause objects to move, face a different direction, or change shape. An object's change in position is called motion. The study of how forces and motions work together is called **mechanics**.

When people push open a door, they apply a force on the door. When children play tug of war, the two teams pull the rope as hard as they can. The pulling puts force on the rope. Force can be weak or strong, but it always tries to cause motion in a certain direction. In a tug of war, each team tries to pull the rope toward its side. The team pulling with the strongest force will make the rope move in its direction.

■ Roller coaster designers use their understanding of forces and motion to create a thrilling ride. They must think about how much force is needed to move the roller coaster up and around the loops without stopping.

The Force of Gravity

Gravity refers to the pull between **masses**. Objects with a high mass have more pull than those with a small mass. This is why large planets have higher gravity than small planets. On Earth, gravity is the force that pulls objects down, toward the center of the planet. When people jump into the air, gravity is the force that pulls them back to the ground.

The strength of an object's gravity depends on the mass of the object. The Moon, for example, has much lower gravity than Earth. When **astronauts** walk on the Moon, they float upward with each step before floating back down to the surface.

■ Astronauts in training learn to work in low-gravity in a special airplane. This airplane flies in a series of roller coaster-like dips and climbs that create brief moments of low gravity for the people on the plane.

The force of gravity gives objects their "weight." Weight is a way of measuring the amount of force gravity places on an object. For example, if an object weighs 50 pounds on Earth, it would only weigh 8 pounds on the Moon. On Jupiter, however, the same object would weigh 118 pounds. This is because Jupiter has a mass equal to about 318 planet Earths.

GRAVITY AND MASS

It can be helpful to think of space as a giant sheet that is pulled flat. Now, imagine a heavy ball is placed on the sheet. The weight of the ball causes the sheet to curve. If a smaller ball is then added, the sheet curves beneath this ball as well. However, the curve under the smaller ball is not as large as the curve under the heavy ball. If the small ball is then rolled toward the heavy ball, the smaller ball falls into the heavy ball's curve and rolls around the heavy ball.

This is how gravity works in outer space. Earth's mass creates a large area of gravity around it. Smaller objects that enter into this area can be pulled by gravity into an **orbit** around the larger object. This is how the Moon orbits Earth.

Frictional Forces

Friction is another common type of force. Friction is the force that works against motion. When a force pushes an object in one direction, friction pushes in the opposite direction.

Friction occurs when two or more objects rub against each other. This is because most surfaces are not perfectly smooth. A kitchen counter may appear smooth, but it is covered in tiny bumps. These bumps may only be visible through a microscope, but they can cause friction. When two surfaces try to move past each other, the bumps on each of the surfaces catch on each other. This causes the motion to slow down.

Objects with a rough surface produce more friction than smooth objects. For this reason, sandpaper rubbing against wood produces more friction than skin rubbing against the inside of a bathtub. Friction is important. Without it, people would not be able to walk, run, turn a door handle, climb stairs, or use a computer mouse.

■ The moving parts in a car engine create friction. The parts are covered with oil to reduce the friction created when they rub against each other.

Types of Friction

There are many types of friction. If objects are not moving, the friction is called **static**. In order to make an object move from a resting position, static friction must be overcome by a stronger force. Moving objects produce **kinetic** friction. There are three main types of kinetic friction.

SLIDING FRICTION

Ice skating is an example of sliding friction. As people skate, their muscles produce the force that allows them to slide along the ice. If they stop pushing and glide, the force of friction will slow them down until they come to a stop.

ROLLING FRICTION

A bowling ball rolling down a bowling lane is an example of rolling friction. Since the surfaces of both the ball and the lane are smooth, the ball moves quickly. A bowling ball would take a long time to slow down. In time, however, it would come to a stop because of friction.

FLUID FRICTION

The friction that occurs when an object moves through air or water is called fluid friction. Fluid friction is what allows people to swim. People use their arms and legs to push against the water and move forward.

Describing Motion

Motion is everywhere. Even when people stand in one place, they are still moving. This is because Earth is always moving. Motion can occur in four ways. An object can move in a straight line, curve in an arc, spin on its **axis**, or move back and forth. Often, motion can be a combination of these movements.

There are three factors to consider when describing motion. The first is the direction of an object's movement. The second is how quickly an object moves from place to place. This is called its **velocity**. The third aspect of motion is how velocity changes over time. This is known as an object's **acceleration**.

When students are walking to school at a constant speed, their velocity is not changing. If they were to hear the school bell ring and realize they were late, they could start running. As they go from walking to running, they increase their velocity, or accelerate.

Skateboarders apply the concepts of force and motion to pull off their tricks. Gravity, rolling friction, and motion all come into play while skateboarding.

Motion can be simple or complex. Simple motion describes an object that moves in a straight line or at a constant velocity. This type of motion is sometimes called uniform motion. Complex motions involve objects that change velocity and direction. This type of motion includes many forces pushing or pulling an object in different directions.

SPEED OR VELOCITY?

Speed and velocity may sound like the same thing, but the two are slightly different. Speed refers only to how fast an object moves from one place to another. Velocity includes both how fast the objects moves and the direction in which it moves. For example, a car's speed could be 100 miles per hour (160 kilometers per hour), but its velocity would be 100 miles per hour (160 km/h) east.

■ Airplane designers must consider all of the forces that will push and pull on the plane while it flies. If these forces are not balanced properly, the plane will not fly.

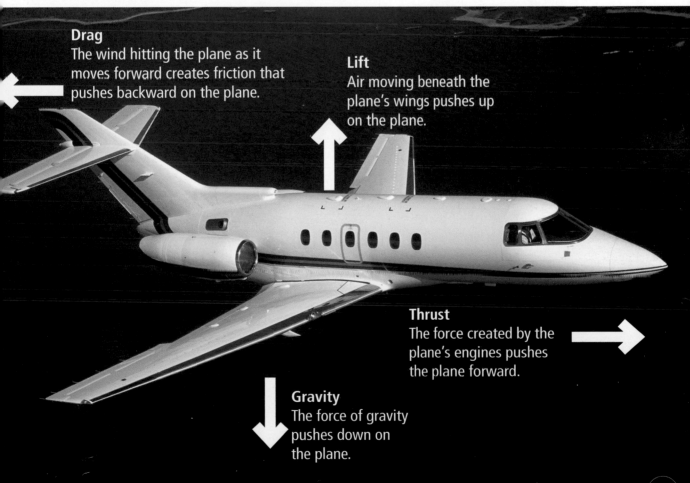

Drag
The wind hitting the plane as it moves forward creates friction that pushes backward on the plane.

Lift
Air moving beneath the plane's wings pushes up on the plane.

Thrust
The force created by the plane's engines pushes the plane forward.

Gravity
The force of gravity pushes down on the plane.

Gravity and Planetary Motion

The force of gravity does not just affect objects on planets. It also affects the planets themselves. The Sun is the largest, or most massive, body in the solar system. This means it has the highest force of gravity. This high force of gravity sets all of the planets in the solar system into their orbits around the Sun and keeps the planets in a constant state of motion.

Sun

Mercury

Venus

Earth

Mars

Jupiter

LEGEND

Path of orbit
around the Sun

WHAT HAVE YOU LEARNED ABOUT PLANETARY MOTION?

This map shows the orbits of planets in Earth's solar system. Use this map, and research online to answer these questions.

1. Which planet takes the longest course around the Sun?
2. Why do these planets stay in their orbits?

Neptune

Uranus

Saturn

First Law of Motion

More than 300 years ago, Isaac Newton discovered three laws of motion that are still used to study **physics**. The first law relates to **inertia**. This law states that objects tend to keep doing what they are already doing. For example, a heavy rock in the middle of a field stays where it is. This is because there are no forces pushing or pulling the rock to make it move from its place.

The rock is said to be in **equilibrium**. This is because the force of gravity pulling it down is balanced by the force of the ground pushing it up. Whenever two forces pushing in opposite directions are the same, the object does not move.

Gravity

Net force

Thrust

■ For a rocket to launch, it must produce enough upward force, called thrust, to overcome the force of gravity. If the force of thrust pushing the rocket up is stronger than the force of gravity pushing the rocket down, the rocket will fly into the air. This is because the overall, or net, force pushes the rocket upward.

Newton's first law also applies to objects that are already in motion. A ball rolling down a hill, for example, will keep rolling unless something stops its motion. In this case, the force of gravity acts on the ball to keep it moving. It keeps doing what it is already doing. However, if the hill levels out, the force of gravity is reduced. Then, the force of rolling friction will bring the ball to a stop.

WHO WAS ISAAC NEWTON?

Isaac Newton (1643–1727) was a British scientist. As a boy, he enjoyed drawing and inventing small machines. When he was older, he studied at Cambridge University. Newton was interested in many subjects, including math, physics, and astronomy.

Newton was the first scientist to describe the force of gravity and the laws of motion. Newton's ideas led to amazing advances in modern physics and engineering.

A story is often told about Newton discovering gravity after an apple fell on his head. The apple did not actually hit Newton on the head, however. Newton once told this story himself. In his own version, he was sitting under a tree and thinking when he saw an apple fall. Newton wondered why apples always fell straight down. This led him to his discoveries about gravity.

NEWTON'S LAWS IN ACTION

Newton's first law of motion is the reason people need to wear seat belts. When a person is traveling in a car at 56 miles per hour (90 km/h) and suddenly puts on the brakes, his or her body tries to keep moving. Without a seat belt, the person's body would continue moving at 56 miles per hour (90 km/h). It would not stop until it crashed into a surface in front of it.

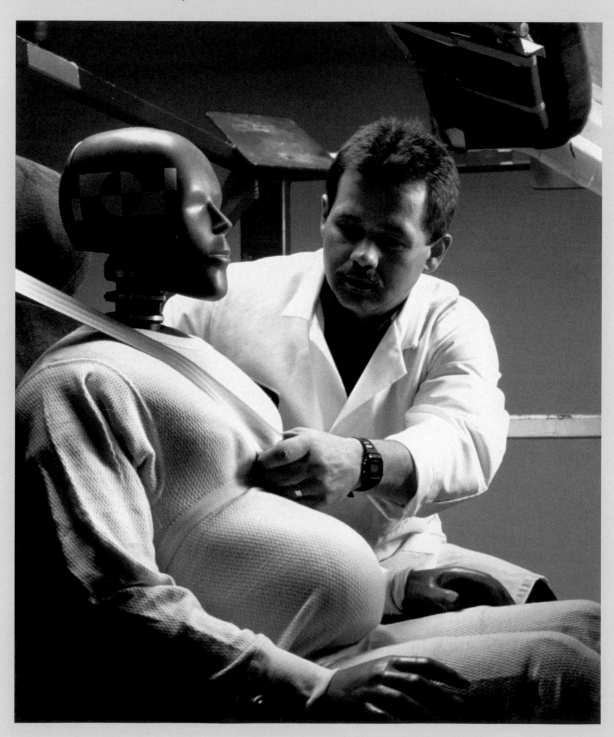

Second Law of Motion

Newton's second law of motion states that an object's acceleration depends on its mass and how much force is applied to it. In math, this is written as F=ma. This means that force is equal to an object's mass multiplied by its acceleration. The law allows people to calculate how much force is needed to move an object at a certain speed. For example, it allows engineers to know how much force an engine will have to produce in order to move a car at a certain speed. It also helps engineers design machines, such as elevators. Elevators must produce enough force to work against gravity, by moving people up, and work with gravity, by moving people down.

■ Newton's second law of motion applies to runners as well. How fast runners can accelerate depends on their mass and how much force they can create with their leg muscles.

Third Law of Motion

Newton's third law deals with the forces that any two objects place on each other. This law states that every action has an equal and opposite reaction.

When two objects interact, they apply forces on each other. When a person sits in a chair, for example, his or her body applies a downward force onto the chair. The chair applies an upward force onto the person's body. These forces are called **action forces** and **reaction forces**. Action and reaction forces control the ways that humans, animals, and machines move in their environment.

■ When rowers paddle a boat, they apply an action force to the water with their paddles. The water applies a reaction force in the opposite direction, which moves the boat forward.

What is a Physicist?

Physicists study **matter**, **energy**, and the way the two interact. Many physicists study subjects such as forces and motion, mechanics, light, heat, and electricity. Some physicists are also engineers. These people design buildings, machines, and bridges.

Physicists work in many fields. Some become university professors, engineers, medical technologists, computer technicians, or city planners. Others work as aerospace engineers, designing aircraft and spacecraft.

Albert Einstein

Albert Einstein (1879–1955) is one of the most influential scientists of the past century. He was born in Germany and later became a Swiss citizen. During World War II, he moved to the United States. Einstein graduated from the University of Zurich with a doctorate degree in physics in 1905. That year, he published four papers that changed human understanding of how the universe operates. He also expanded on Isaac Newton's theory of gravity.

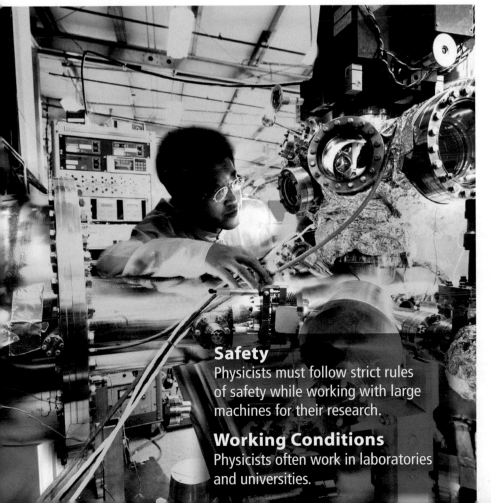

Safety
Physicists must follow strict rules of safety while working with large machines for their research.

Working Conditions
Physicists often work in laboratories and universities.

Six Facts About Forces and Motion

Ignoring friction from air, Earth's gravity causes falling objects to accelerate by 32 feet per second (9.8 meters per second) every second.

Roller coasters can cause riders to experience forces up to six times the force of gravity, or 6 g-forces.

The world's fastest land mammal is the cheetah. This cat can accelerate from zero to more than 60 miles per hour (100 km/h) in a few seconds.

Speed skating is the fastest sport in the world that is fully human powered. Skaters can reach speeds of more than 37 miles per hour (60 km/h).

The fastest human in the world is Jamaican Usain Bolt, who holds the record for running 100 meters in 9.58 seconds.

Astronauts who stay in space for long periods of time grow taller. This is because there is little gravity pushing down on them in space.

Forces and Motion
Brain Teasers

1 The pull between two objects is called what type of force?

2 A soccer ball slowing down as it rolls on grass is an example of what type of force?

3 When a runner trips on a rock and falls forward, this is an example of what type of force?

4 What is the main source of the ocean's tides?

5 Do objects on the Moon weigh more or less than they do on Earth? Why?

6 Which of Newton's three laws of motion can be used to determine how fast an object can accelerate?

7 A lack of which force would cause a person's foot to slip when stepping into a bathtub?

8 What kind of measurement is used to describe an object moving west at 50 miles per hour (80 km/h)?

9 What are the two main types of friction?

10 Which two forces are described by Newton's third law of motion?

ANSWERS: 1. Gravity 2. Friction 3. Inertia 4. Gravitational pull of the Sun and Moon 5. Less. The pull of gravity is lower on the Moon than on Earth. 6. Newton's Second Law 7. Friction 8. Velocity 9. Static and kinetic 10. Action and reaction

21

Science in Action

Buckle Up!

Follow these simple instructions to demonstrate Newton's first law of motion as it applies to seat belts.

Tools Needed

Five or six thick books

A piece of wood or stiff cardboard

Modeling clay

A toy car

String

Directions

1 Use the books and the wood or cardboard to make a ramp. Place one book at the bottom of the ramp to form a barrier that the toy car will run into.

2 Use the clay to make a model of a person sitting down. Place the model inside or on top of the car.

3 Place the toy car at the top of the ramp. What do you think will happen to the clay model when the car reaches the bottom of the ramp?

4 Release the toy car. Did the car crash at the bottom of the ramp? What happened to the clay model?

5 Use the string to tie the model to the car, and repeat steps 3 and 4 again. What happens?

6 What difference did the string make? What does this tell you about wearing a seat belt when you ride in a car?

Words to Know

acceleration: the rate of change of velocity, or speed, over time

action forces: the force pulling or pushing in one direction; opposite to the direction of the reaction force

astronauts: people trained to explore space

axis: an imaginary line through the center of an object around which the object rotates

energy: the ability to do work

equilibrium: the state of two opposite forces balancing and canceling each other out

friction: the force that resists the motion of one surface relative to another with which it is in contact; caused by the tiny surface bumps on the two surfaces catching on each other

gravity: the force that pulls two or more objects with mass toward each other

inertia: the tendency of an object to remain in the same state of motion or rest

kinetic: force that results from the motion of an object

masses: the amount of matter contained in objects; combine with gravity to produce an object's weight

matter: anything that has mass and takes up space

mechanics: the study of forces and motion

orbit: the curved path of objects around heavier objects, such as the Moon's path around Earth

physicists: scientists that study physics

physics: the study of matter and energy and their interactions

reaction forces: the force pulling or pushing in another direction; opposite to the direction of the action force

renewable energy: energy that comes from sources that can be used again and again, such as wind or solar power

static: the force of friction that works to keep objects at rest from moving

tide: the rise and fall of the water level in seas, oceans, and large lakes

turbines: engines with rotating fan blades that convert the movement of air or water into electricity

velocity: the distance an object covers in a set period of time in a certain direction

Index

acceleration 10, 17, 20, 21
action 5, 18, 21

Einstein, Albert 19
equilibrium 14

force 4, 5, 6, 7, 8, 9, 10, 11, 12, 14, 15, 17, 18, 19, 20, 21

friction 8, 9, 10, 11, 15, 20, 21

gravity 6, 7, 10, 11, 12, 14, 15, 17, 19, 20, 21

mass 6, 7, 17

Newton, Isaac 14, 15, 16, 17, 18, 19, 21, 22

physicist 19
physics 14, 15, 19

reaction 18, 21

speed 10, 11, 17, 20

tide 4, 21

velocity 10, 11, 21

Log on to www.av2books.com

AV² by Weigl brings you media enhanced books that support active learning. Go to www.av2books.com, and enter the special code found on page 2 of this book. You will gain access to enriched and enhanced content that supplements and complements this book. Content includes video, audio, web links, quizzes, a slide show, and activities.

Audio
Listen to sections of the book read aloud.

Video
Watch informative video clips.

Embedded Weblinks
Gain additional information for research.

Try This!
Complete activities and hands-on experiments.

WHAT'S ONLINE?

Try This!	Embedded Weblinks	Video	EXTRA FEATURES
Test your knowledge about types of friction.	Review of the basics of forces and motion.	Watch a video introduction to forces and motion.	**Audio** Listen to sections of the book read aloud.
Identify uses of forces and motion in the United States.	Find out more information about specific topics in forces and motion.	Watch another video about forces and motion.	**Key Words** Study vocabulary, and complete a matching word activity.
Add your own facts to the fact section.	Explore interactive learning tools.		**Slide Show** View images and captions, and prepare a presentation.
Find out more about forces and motion through an educational activity.	Learn more about the uses of forces and motion in the United States.		**Quizzes** Test your knowledge.
	Discover more about the history of forces and motion.		
	Read about an important scientist.		

AV² was built to bridge the gap between print and digital. We encourage you to tell us what you like and what you want to see in the future.
Sign up to be an AV² Ambassador at www.av2books.com/ambassador.